Guess the Covered Word for Seasons and Holidays

by
Dorothy P. Hall
and
Marie C. Daniel

Carson-Dellosa Publishing Company, Inc.
Greensboro, North Carolina

Editors
Sabena Maiden
Joey Bland

Cover Design
Matthew Van Zomeren

Layout Design
Jon Nawrocik

Inside Illustrations
Mike Duggins

DEDICATION

This book is dedicated to the memory of Charlie Cross—Marie's father, my friend and a friend to all the teachers and children who knew him. He was a volunteer at Clemmons Elementary (his daughter's school) and Bolton Elementary (his wife's school) for many years. Charlie Cross was always present on holidays, bringing the turkey to feed a class, or helping in any way he could with the celebrations. Marie was a student at Clemmons, a student teacher at Clemmons, and is teaching at Clemmons now. Charlie encouraged Marie to become a teacher like her mother, Carol Cross.

Charlie Cross also encouraged me in my early work with Four-Blocks at Clemmons Elementary. He was so proud of Marie's "open door" to visitors and all the wonderful things they said about her Four-Blocks teaching. Marie has had visitors during all the blocks, but she usually does the Working with Words Block for visitors. She chooses this block because (1) she does it so well, and (2) she likes Working with Words and it shows.

Charlie's family and friends miss him. He was truly a friend to educators and education and all who knew him. He would be so proud of this book—another accomplishment of his daughter, Marie Cross Daniel.

Dottie Hall

This book is dedicated to my two children. To my daughter, Carlie, who is named after her grandmother Carol and her grandfather Charlie Cross, and to my son, William Lee Daniel IV (whom we call Ivy).

Marie Daniel

TABLE OF CONTENTS

LESSONS

Seasons and Holidays Lessons
September

October

November

TRANSPARENCIES

Seasons and Holidays Lessons
September

October

November

INTRODUCTION

Guess the Covered Word is a popular Working with Words activity in Four-Blocks classrooms (Cunningham & Hall, 1996; Hall & Cunningham, 1997; Cunningham and Hall, 1997; and Cunningham, Hall, and Sigmon, 1998). Its purpose is to help children practice the important strategy of cross-checking meaning with letter sound information. Some children never become really good at putting sounds together to decode a word, but most words can be figured out by students if they look at the beginning letters, check the length of the word, and think about what word would make sense in the sentence. It is this cross-checking ability that Guess the Covered Word activities help children develop. For some children, this is their most successful decoding activity. For many children, this decoding activity is fun. It provides children with a strategy that is easy to remember and use when they are reading independently and come to a word they do not know.

When we read, we recognize most words immediately and automatically because we have seen and read them before. When we do see new words—words we have never encountered in reading before—we figure them out. Many words can be figured out by thinking about what would make sense in a sentence and seeing if the consonants in the word match what you are thinking of. The ability to use the consonants in a word, along with the context, is called cross-checking, and it is an important decoding strategy. Children must learn to do two things simultaneously: think about what would make sense and think about letters and sounds. Most children would prefer to do one or the other but not both. Thus, some children guess something that is sensible but ignore the letter sounds they know. Other children guess something that is close to the sounds but makes no sense in the sentence.

Our Class

Here is the procedure for Guess the Covered Word, explained with the warm-up lessons that you can use when introducing the activity to your students.

(1) Display four or five sentences on a large piece of chart paper, the board, or on an overhead transparency. (We have done the lessons on transparencies.) Cover a word in each sentence using two self-stick notes—one to cover the onset (all of the consonants before the first vowel) and the other to cover the rest of the word. You may wish to cut or tear the self-stick notes so that the children become aware of the length of the word. Many teachers also like to purchase dark colored self-stick notes (black is best), so that the covered words don't show through.

Lesson 1 is located on the top of the first transparency. It has lines at the beginning of the sentence on which to write your students' names and another line at the end of the sentence to write the things they like to do (the covered words). This first activity is best done with your students' names and what they like to do because it will get students involved and make the activity more meaningful and fun.

(2) Let the children read each sentence, then make several guesses for the covered word. Point out to the students that there are generally many possibilities for a word that will fit the context when they can't see any of the letters. Write the guesses next to the sentence on chart paper, the board, or the transparency. This way, you can refer to potentially correct responses as you move through the three steps of the strategy. (Four or five guesses are enough. Any more than that will make the activity take too long!)

(3) Next, take off the first self-stick note, which always covers all of the letters up to the first vowel. Together with the class, look to see if any of the guesses begin the same way. Eliminate the guesses that don't begin with the correct letter and add new guesses that fit the meaning and start with the right beginning letter.

(4) When you've written all of the guesses that fit both meaning and beginning sound, and you've encouraged students to think about the length of the word, remove the second self-stick note to reveal the whole word.

5) Use this same procedure with the remaining sentences.

With just 4-5 sentences, it does not take long to do this activity, and young children have fun learning an important decoding strategy.

Here is another set of sentences found on the bottom of the first transparency to practice Guess the Covered Word.

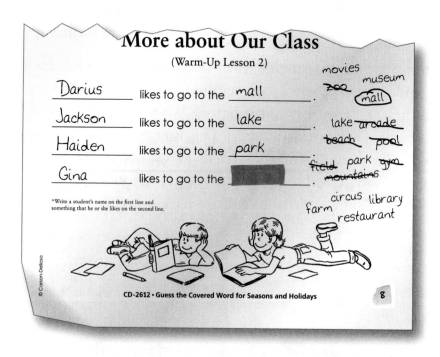

As students share their guesses, list them on chart paper, the board, or the transparency.

Our Teacher

Another popular Guess the Covered Word activity to do when school first starts is to write about the teacher (YOU!). Children like to learn about their new teachers, and what an enjoyable way to give this information to them. Here are some sentences used by one teacher to introduce this activity to her second-graders. (Write your own sentences about yourself, and your children will love getting to know you!)

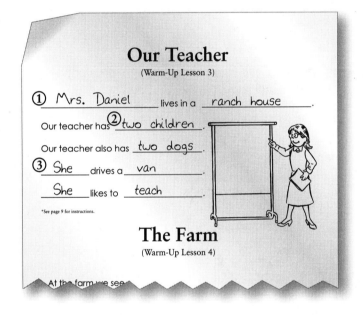

① Insert your name and change house to apartment or condo, if needed.

② If you have two, three, four, etc., of anything (brothers, dogs, children, etc.) then write the number before the covered word. If not, just write the covered word.

③ Use he or she as needed.

You should only cover words with a single beginning consonant in the first Guess the Covered Word lessons, but soon include words that begin with letter combinations, such as *c-h* and *b-r*. The lesson above has one word that begins with *ch* and one covered word that is not the last word in the sentence. However, don't completely move away from including some words with single beginning consonants.

As students share their guesses, list them on chart paper, the board, or the transparency.

The Farm

Be sure that when you uncover the beginning letters, you uncover all of the letters in front of the vowel. If you have uncovered a *b* and a child guesses the word *brick*, tell the child that was good thinking for the *b*. Then, have everyone say *brick* slowly so that they hear the *b* and *r* at the beginning of the word. Remind students that when you uncovered the beginning letter(s), you revealed all of the letters in front of the vowel. If the word were *brick*, there would also be an *r* revealed. Here are some starter sentences for two-letter combinations:

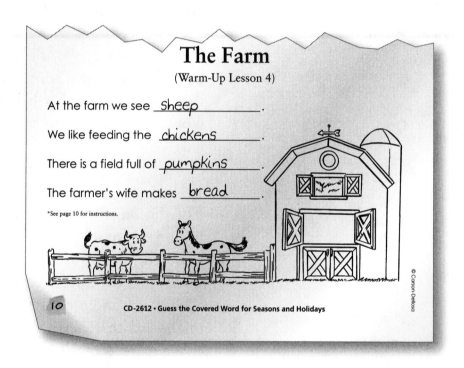

The Farm
(Warm-Up Lesson 4)

At the farm we see ___sheep___ .

We like feeding the ___chickens___ .

There is a field full of ___pumpkins___ .

The farmer's wife makes ___bread___ .

*See page 10 for instructions.

CD-2612 • Guess the Covered Word for Seasons and Holidays

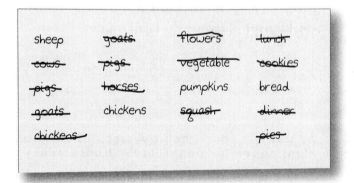

sheep	~~goats~~	~~flowers~~	~~lunch~~
~~cows~~	~~pigs~~	~~vegetable~~	~~cookies~~
~~pigs~~	~~horses~~	pumpkins	bread
~~goats~~	chickens	~~squash~~	~~dinner~~
~~chickens~~			~~pies~~

As students share their guesses, list them on chart paper, the board, or the transparency.

What Do You Like to Eat?

As you can see, Guess the Covered Word lessons provide review of beginning letter sounds for those who still need it in the primary grades. The most sophisticated readers are consolidating the important strategy of using meaning, all of the beginning letters, and word length as clues to identify an unknown word. Guess the Covered Word is an activity in which you teach and remind the children that guessing based only on a single criterion (the first letters, the length of a word, or the word that makes sense) won't help them figure out many words in their reading. Guessing a word using all three cues is a much more reliable method, and this approach will help students correctly identify the word more often than not. Following are some sentences to use when reviewing this approach. In first grade, 4–5 sentences are all that you need to do at one time; three more have been added for the second- and third-grade classes. (Remember to use your students' names in the sentences.)

As students share their guesses, list them on chart paper, the board, or the transparency.

Our School

In the first Guess the Covered Word lessons, only words at the ends of the sentences are covered. Later, covered words occur anywhere in the sentences. See the sample sentences below to try with your class. (Use your school name on the line and choose covered words appropriate to your school. These words will work for most.)

Our School

(Warm-Up Lesson 6)

Our school is ___big___.

Lots of _children_ go to _Clemmons Elementary._

The ___principal___ watches us get off the bus.

We must walk in the _halls_____.

Many _teachers_ work at school.

*See page 12 for instructions.

WELCOME STUDENTS!

CD-2612 • Guess the Covered Word for Seasons and Holidays   12

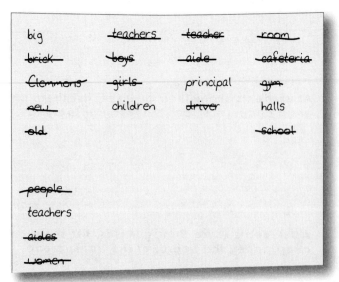

big	~~teachers~~	~~teacher~~	~~room~~
~~brick~~	~~boys~~	~~aide~~	~~cafeteria~~
~~Clemmons~~	~~girls~~	principal	~~gym~~
~~new~~	children	~~driver~~	halls
~~old~~			~~school~~
~~people~~			
teachers			
~~aides~~			
~~women~~			

As students share their guesses, list them on chart paper, the board, or the transparency.

© Carson-Dellosa

Sylvester and the Magic Pebble

Teachers in second and third grades need to do some lessons in which the covered words occur in paragraphs taken from stories or informational books. This is how most students will encounter unknown words when they are reading. Each sentence in the paragraph has a word to be guessed that is covered with the usual two self-stick notes. Read the paragraph one sentence at a time and allow students to make guesses for each covered word. As you progress through the paragraph, students should use the whole context of what has been read so far to figure out each new covered word. Be sure to have your self-stick notes cut to size so that word length is obvious, and when you remove the first self-stick note, show the children all of the letters up to the vowel. Here is a summary of a story (Lesson 7).

Sylvester and the Magic Pebble

By William Steig

(Warm-Up Lesson 7)

Sylvester collects pebbles of all **colors**. One day, Sylvester finds a **special** pebble that can make wishes come true. On the way home, he is **frightened** by a lion. Instead of wishing the lion was a **butterfly**, Sylvester wishes he was a stone. Meanwhile, his **parents** are worried when he doesn't come home. They ask the **children** if they have seen Sylvester. His parents cannot find him and are **miserable**. One day they go on a **picnic** and find the magic pebble. They put it on the **big** stone nearby. Sylvester wishes to be **himself** again, and it happens. Now everyone in the family has just what they **want**!

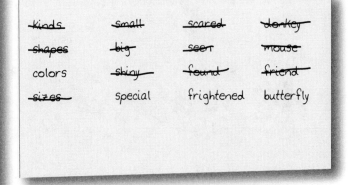

~~kinds~~	~~small~~	~~scared~~	~~donkey~~
~~shapes~~	~~big~~	~~seen~~	~~mouse~~
colors	~~shiny~~	~~found~~	~~friend~~
~~sizes~~	special	frightened	butterfly

As students share their guesses, list them on chart paper, the board, or the transparency.

Sea Horses

Following is an informational article (Lesson 8) to practice Guess the Covered Word using a paragraph. Remember to read one sentence at a time and allow students to make guesses for each covered word.

Sea Horses
(Warm-Up Lesson 8)

Sea horses are **fish**. A sea horse has a long **snout**. It sucks **food** into a toothless mouth. Its eyes **swivel** so it can watch its prey without moving. A very unusual fact is that father sea horses have the **babies**. **Crabs** eat sea horses. People catch them and use them in **medicine**. If people keep **catching** sea horses, they could become extinct!

~~small~~	~~tail~~	~~water~~	~~open~~
fish	~~nose~~	food	~~see~~
~~pretty~~	~~fin~~	~~things~~	~~shake~~
~~cute~~	~~life~~	~~stuff~~	~~move~~
~~nice~~	snout	~~fish~~	swivel

As students share their guesses, list them on chart paper, the board, or the transparency.

For Guess the Covered Word lessons, you can use pages from big books you are reading, story summaries, themes you are studying, or information about holidays and seasons. You can write sentences and paragraphs with covered words in various locations. Two kinds of Guess the Covered Word lessons are included in this book. Easy lessons are on the top of each transparency. Here you will find 4-5 sentences for first grade and beginning readers in second and third grades. The bottom half of the transparency is on the same topic, but written in paragraph form. These paragraphs are for second- and third-grade teachers to use. Note that most of the transparencies contain two lessons, so when doing a lesson, cover the other lesson with a sheet of paper.

GUESS THE COVERED WORD

In order to help children cross check meaning with sound:

(1) First, have students guess the word with no letters showing. The missing word is covered entirely with self-stick notes, one for the beginning letters and one for the rest of the word. There are generally many possibilities for a word that will fit the context. Write four or five guesses.

(2) Next, pull off the first self-stick note, revealing the letters up to the vowel and limiting the possibilities. The children may have to make additional guesses if none of their original guesses are correct.

(3) Finally, show the whole word and help children confirm which guess makes sense and has the right letters.

REFERENCES

Cunningham, P. M. & Hall, D. P. (1997) *Month-by-Month Phonics for First Grade.* Greensboro, NC: Carson-Dellosa.

Cunningham, P. M. & Hall, D. P. (1998) *Month-by-Month Phonics for Third Grade.* Greensboro, NC: Carson-Dellosa.

Cunningham, P. M., Hall, D. P. and Sigmon, C. M. (1999) *The Teacher's Guide to the Four-Blocks.* Greensboro, NC: Carson-Dellosa.

Hall, D. P. & Cunningham, P. M. (1998) *Month-by-Month Phonics for Second Grade.* Greensboro, NC: Carson-Dellosa.

Children's Book Cited
Sylvester and the Magic Pebble by William Steig (Simon & Schuster, 1988).

September

Back to School By September, children are in school, ready to learn all of the new and exciting knowledge their teachers have to share.

Johnny Appleseed Born John Chapman on September 26, 1774, Johnny Appleseed is well-known for planting apple seeds throughout much of the United States. A popular folk hero, many teachers incorporate his story into their back-to-school lessons when apple themes are very popular.

Grandparents' Day Celebrated the first Sunday after Labor Day, this day originated in 1973 as a way to honor the elderly in the United States. It provides opportunities for children to understand the valuable contributions the elderly have made.

October

Fall This season begins on the autumnal equinox, which occurs on September 22 or 23. Many teachers celebrate fall with their students in October, since it is the first full month of this season.

Jack-O'-Lantern During the month of October, there are school fall festivals and festive parties with pumpkin-carving activities and costume-making for Halloween, which is on October 31.

November

Pumpkins As fall continues into November, pumpkins can still be seen everywhere. Recipes and activities—all made with pumpkins—are perfect for fall units and celebrations.

Thanksgiving This holiday, which takes place in the United States the fourth Thursday in November, is a time for friends and families to come together to share food and give thanks for the year's blessings. It acknowledges the first Thanksgiving celebrated by the Pilgrims.

December

December Holidays There are many holidays in December. Three of the most commonly celebrated holidays are Christmas, Hanukkah, and Kwanzaa. This is the perfect time of year for teachers to explain to students the diversity of cultures and variety of celebrations that take place during this month.

Christmas December 25 is Christmas. It originated as a Christian holiday to observe the birth of Jesus Christ. While Christmas traditions and celebrations vary by family, Santa Claus visits many homes to give presents to adoring children.

Hanukkah This Jewish holiday begins the twenty-fifth day of the Hebrew month of Kislev, which falls in November or December. Lasting eight days, The Festival of Lights recognizes the victory of a group of Jewish soldiers who fought for religious freedom.

Kwanzaa Occurring December 26 through January 1, Kwanzaa is honored by many African-Americans. Lasting for seven days, this holiday was created to celebrate African traditions and culture.

January

Winter Beginning on the winter solstice on December 21st or 22nd, this season often contains themes about wintry weather and activities.

New Year's Day The first day of the new year is January 1. Many people "ring in the new year" with parties and activities on New Year's Eve, which is December 31. Traditionally during the first week of January, many people relax and reflect, planning their resolutions for the upcoming year.

Martin Luther King, Jr. A man who worked very hard to establish peace and justice was Martin Luther King, Jr. Born January 15, 1944, this leader of the U.S. Civil Rights movement is honored the third Monday in January.

February

Groundhog Day Every year on February 2, Punxsutawney Phil emerges from his burrow in Pennsylvania. If he sees his shadow, there will be six more weeks of winter weather. This event makes for a great unit on weather, animals, and legends.

Valentine's Day On February 14, Valentine's Day is celebrated. Although the origination of this special day is inconclusive, today, many people give their special loved ones a paper valentine or candy. This provides students a chance to show their classmates how much they love working together to learn.

Presidents' Day The third Monday in February is set aside to honor the office of the president of the United States of America, as well as two early presidents, George Washington and Abraham Lincoln. George Washington, born February 22, 1732, became the first president of the United States in 1789. Because he was the first president, George Washington is one of the most recognized by students. Abraham Lincoln, the fourteenth president of the United States, was born February 12, 1809. Lincoln is well-known for issuing the Emancipation Proclamation to abolish slavery. Social studies lessons can be enhanced with the study of the great leaders of the United States.

March

St. Patrick's Day On March 17, Saint Patrick, the patron saint of Ireland, is honored. In Ireland, this holiday is mostly a religious observation, but in many other countries, the holiday is acknowledged with festive parties and parades. Many students wear green in order to avoid a pinch from a classmate.

Wind In many places, the month of March is often windy. This month is perfect to enhance science units about the weather and to create art projects with kites.

April

Easter This holiday falls on the first Sunday following the paschal full moon (the first ecclesiastical full moon that occurs on or after the day of the vernal equinox), which means Easter can never occur before March 22 or later than April 25. Christians remember this day to acknowledge Christ's resurrection. Many people celebrate the day with the Easter Bunny's candy and egg hunts.

Spring This season begins on the vernal equinox which occurs on March 20 or 21. April is a great month to teach lessons about spring as flowers bloom and many animals are born.

May

Mother's Day This holiday, celebrated the second Sunday in May, is a day set aside to acknowledge mothers and to thank them for the many wonderful things they do.

Memorial Day The last Monday in May is Memorial Day. This is a day to honor those who have died serving the United States in war.

June

Father's Day This holiday, celebrated the third Sunday in June, is a day to thank fathers for the many wonderful things they do throughout year.

Summer Beginning on the summer solstice on June 21 or 22, this season is often learned about in June before students go home for summer break.

Our Class

(Warm-Up Lesson 1)

_____ likes _____.

_____ likes _____.

_____ likes _____.

_____ likes _____.

*Write a student's name on the first line and
something that he or she likes on the second line.

More about Our Class

(Warm-Up Lesson 2)

_____ likes to go to the _____.

_____ likes to go to the _____.

_____ likes to go to the _____.

_____ likes to go to the _____.

*Write a student's name on the first line and
something that he or she likes on the second line.

Our Teacher

(Warm-Up Lesson 3)

_____ lives in a _____.

Our teacher has _____ .

Our teacher also has _____ .

_____ drives a _____ .

_____ likes to _____ .

*See page 9 for instructions.

The Farm

(Warm-Up Lesson 4)

At the farm we see _____ .

We like feeding the _____ .

There is a field full of _____ .

The farmer's wife makes _____ .

*See page 10 for instructions.

What Do You Like to Eat?

(Warm-Up Lesson 5)

_____ likes _____ .

_____ likes _____ .

_____ likes _____ .

_____ likes _____ .

_____ likes _____ .

*Write a student's name on the first line and
something that he or she likes to eat on the second line.

Our School

(Warm-Up Lesson 6)

Our school is _____ .

Lots of _____ go to _____ .

The _____ watches us get off the bus.

We must walk in the _____ .

Many _____ work at school.

*See page 12 for instructions.

WELCOME STUDENTS!

Sylvester and the Magic Pebble

By William Steig

(Warm-Up Lesson 7)

Sylvester collects pebbles of all **colors**. One day, Sylvester finds a **special** pebble that can make wishes come true. On the way home, he is **frightened** by a lion. Instead of wishing the lion was a **butterfly**, Sylvester wishes he was a stone. Meanwhile, his **parents** are worried when he doesn't come home. They ask the **children** if they have seen Sylvester. His parents cannot find him and are **miserable**. One day they go on a **picnic** and find the magic pebble. They put it on the **big** stone nearby. Sylvester wishes to be **himself** again, and it happens. Now everyone in the family has just what they **want**!

Sea Horses

(Warm-Up Lesson 8)

Sea horses are **fish**. A sea horse has a long **snout**. It sucks **food** into a toothless mouth. Its eyes **swivel** so it can watch its prey without moving. A very unusual fact is that father sea horses have the **babies**. **Crabs** eat sea horses. People catch them and use them in **medicine**. If people keep **catching** sea horses, they could become extinct!

Back to School

Boys and girls are back in school.

Some have new **notebooks**.

Some have new **backpacks**.

In them are paper and **pencils**.

To color, they have **markers**.

Back to School

Children and teachers are back in school. Many children ride **buses** to school. Other children can walk. Some children carry a new **notebook**. Other children have a new **backpack**. In it they have notebooks and **pencils**. Many children wear new **clothes** to school. Some children bring a favorite **book** to school. At school you meet new **friends**. What will we learn this year in **school**?

Johnny Appleseed

Johnny Appleseed was a friend to **animals**.

Johnny Appleseed was a **kind** man.

People liked to hear his **stories**.

People liked his apple **plants**.

Johnny Appleseed

Johnny Appleseed lived long ago. He was born and grew up in **Massachusetts**. His **home** was surrounded with apple trees. He liked **nature**. He traveled **west**. He planted apple trees along the **way**. Johnny liked to tell **stories**. Johnny Appleseed is a **folk** hero today.

Grandparents' Day

My grandma and I like to **cook**.

I make **banana** pudding with my grandma.

My granddad and I like to play **cards**.

My grandparents' **hugs** are the best!

Grandparents' Day

The first Sunday in September is Grandparents' Day. Some children have just a **grandmother**. Other children have both **sets** of grandparents. Many people get their grandparents a special **card**. It is nice when we can spend time with our **grandparents**. My family plans to **buy** a special card. We will also cook their favorite **meal**. We like shopping for a **present**, also. We will spend the **weekend** together. It will be **fun** for all. It is always a special day.

Fall

Green leaves are changing **colors**.

Children like to dress up in funny **costumes**.

In the field are **pumpkins**.

Many schools have fall **festivals**.

Fall

October is a **fall** month. The days are getting **cooler**. The nights are getting **longer**. Homes and schools are decorated with **pumpkins**. Children often wear **costumes** in October. They get **candy** from friends. Children sometimes visit **haunted** houses. Many schools have a fall **festival**. There are many **strange** sights to see in October.

Jack-O'-Lantern

My jack-o'-lantern has **yellow** eyes.

It has a **tiny** nose.

His face is **smiling**.

I made him with **pointed** teeth.

Jack-O'-Lantern

A **church** in my neighborhood was selling pumpkins. My **family** bought one to make a jack-o'-lantern. We carved **triangles** for eyes. Then, we cut a **round** nose. Last, we gave him four **pointed** teeth. His face looks **funny** with a candle burning inside. We will put him on the **porch** for all to see.

Pumpkins

Pumpkins grow in **gardens**.

They come in all **sizes**.

Some are used for **cooking**.

We see pumpkins in **stores**.

Pumpkins

Pumpkins come in many **shapes**. Farmers plant pumpkin seeds in the **spring**. First, the **vines** appear. Gold-colored flowers begin to **bloom** next. A small pumpkin's skin is green, and then it turns **orange**. In the fall they are ready to harvest and sell at **stores**.

Thanksgiving

Mom will buy a **turkey** to cook.

Corn is my favorite vegetable.

We will have **pumpkin** pie.

Dad watches **football** on television.

Thanksgiving

The Pilgrims came to America on the *Mayflower*. It was not a **big** ship. It was a long, hard **voyage**. Most people did not have a lot of **clothes**. The Pilgrims were glad to reach **shore**. The natives helped them **hunt**. The natives taught the Pilgrims how to plant **pumpkins**. When it was fall, it was time for the first **harvest**. The Pilgrims hunted for **turkey**. The women cooked **vegetables**. The children picked **blueberries** and played games. The Pilgrims had the first Thanksgiving **feast** long ago.

December Holidays

December is a **busy** month.

People are getting ready for the **holidays**.

They cook **favorite** foods.

They buy **gifts** for family and friends.

Homes are decorated with **candles**.

December Holidays

December is a **special** month. People all over the **world** have holidays they celebrate. In the United States, many people celebrate **Christmas**, **Hanukkah**, or **Kwanzaa**. We decorate our **homes**. Many people put decorations on their **doors**. On the **streets** we see pretty lights. People are **shopping**. I buy gifts for my **family**. We make delicious **treats** to give our friends. We sing songs at **school**. We try to learn about different **customs**.

Christmas

It is a family tradition to **shop** on Christmas Eve.

We **bake** cookies while Mom wraps presents.

Dad drives us around so we can see the **lights**.

We leave Santa Claus a **cookie** before we go to bed.

I like the **gifts** the best.

Hanukkah

Grace likes to get **toys** for Hanukkah.

Mel likes to get **money** best of all.

My **mother** always lights the menorah.

We light the menorah at **supper** time.

Candles are also a common symbol for Christmas and Kwanzaa.

Kwanzaa

Kwanzaa started so African-Americans would learn more about their **roots**. People gather **seven** symbols to display in their homes for the holiday. Most people begin by lighting the **black** candle on the first night of Kwanzaa for unity. On the second day, self-determination is celebrated by lighting the **red** candle. Each night they light a candle to remind people of important **principles**. Families eat **special** foods to bring them good luck. Everybody **rejoices** during the Kwanzaa celebration.

Winter

Heidi has a new **coat** to keep her warm.

Gary likes to play in the **snow**.

Haley has fun making a **snowman**.

Jackson wears a **scarf** in the snow.

Thad plays **hockey** with his friends.

Winter

In many places, January is a cold **month**. It is winter, and snow is on the **ground**. Days are **short**, and nights are long. Snow **falls**, and it is cold. People wear **warm** clothes and stay inside. The birds have flown **south** for the winter. Some animals **hibernate**. Other animals **hunt** for food. When it is below **freezing** for many days, the children can go ice-skating on lakes and ponds. When it snows, children make snowmen and go **sliding** down hills on sleds. They dress warmly and have fun outside.

New Year's Day

January 1 begins a new **year**.

Many people make New Year's **resolutions**.

Some try to break **old** habits.

Some try to start better **lives**.

New Year's Day

Many people have a **celebration** on New Year's Eve. They stay up until **midnight**. They like to **dance** and eat. I like to wear my best **clothes**. Many people eat **greens** on New Year's Day. Some people try to give up **bad** habits. They hope that this year they will live **healthier** lives. Everyone **shouts**, "Happy New Year!" to family and friends.

Martin Luther King, Jr.

Martin Luther King, Jr. was a great **leader**.

He spent his life **fighting** for civil rights.

He dreamed of a world free of **hate**.

Many people **remember** Martin Luther King, Jr.

Martin Luther King, Jr.

Martin Luther King, Jr. was born in 1929 in Atlanta, Georgia. His father was a minister, and his mother was a **teacher**. As a boy, he learned that because of the color of his skin, he did not have the same **rights** as other people. In many places, he could not eat at the same **restaurants** as white people. He dreamed of a world free of **prejudice**. Martin Luther King, Jr. spent his life **fighting** for civil rights. He met with presidents and led peaceful **marches**. He was **killed** in Memphis, Tennessee, in 1968. He was a great **leader**. He left behind millions of tearful Americans who **respected** him.

Groundhog Day

Groundhogs are found in many **places**.

Groundhogs **sleep** in winter.

Each **year** we see if the groundhog sees his shadow.

If he does, there will be more **winter** weather.

Groundhog Day

The groundhog is found in many **states**. They **hibernate** in winter. On February 2, **people** watch to see if the groundhog sees his shadow. It started long ago in Europe as **farmers** watched to see if the animals saw their shadows on February 2. In the United States, it began in Pennsylvania when people hiked to the **burrow** of Phil the Groundhog to see if he saw his shadow. If the day was sunny, he would see his shadow, and he would return to his **den** for six more weeks. If the day was cloudy, he would not see his shadow, and spring would soon arrive. Now, you hear about it on the **news**. Everyone **watches** to see what happens on Groundhog Day.

Valentine's Day

Charlie likes to give **flowers** to his mom.

Ivy keeps the valentines in a **box**.

Carol gives **cards** to her friends.

Lee hopes to get **candy** from his friends.

Carlie puts **stickers** on her valentines.

Valentine's Day

For Valentine's Day, I mail cards to my **grandma**. At school we have a **celebration**. The room is decorated with **hearts**. We make **valentines** with colored paper, glue, and glitter. The cards go in a special **box**. We eat **cupcakes** and drink red punch. My family gives me **candy** with messages that say, "I love you!" Some people get **gifts** for Valentine's Day.

Presidents' Day

George Washington was a **soldier** in the Revolutionary War.

He wore a **white** wig.

He was the first **president** of the United States.

Abraham Lincoln walked miles to get **books**.

He was a **lawyer** when he grew up.

Lincoln was the **leader** during the American Civil War.

George Washington

George Washington liked to ride his horse and go **boating**. His favorite subject was **math**. He learned how to **survey** the land. He married and moved to Mount Vernon, a **home** in Virginia. A **war** broke out between England and the American colonies. George Washington was a **hero** during the American Revolution. He was **chosen** to be the first president of the United States. A **capital** was built and named after him. George Washington was a great **leader**.

Abraham Lincoln

Abraham Lincoln was born in a **log** cabin. He loved **reading** as a boy. He grew up to be a lawyer. Lincoln was **president** during the American Civil War. He was a **caring** leader. He wanted all **Americans** to be free. The war lasted **many** years. The North finally won, and **slavery** was not allowed anymore. Lincoln was **killed** in a theater before he finished his presidency.

St. Patrick's Day

We went to a St. Patrick's Day **parade**.

I wore my green **hat**.

Shannon saw a **leprechaun**.

The leprechaun hid under a **mushroom**.

It's fun to **hunt** for leprechauns on St. Patrick's Day.

St. Patrick's Day

Long ago, Ireland had many **snakes**. They were everywhere!
People did not like this. St. Patrick drove the snakes from Ireland
into the **sea**. Soon, the **Irish** started celebrating St. Patrick's Day.
In many cities, there are **parades**. People wear green and have
special **parties**. They tell stories about **leprechauns**. People
color their food and **drinks** green. In some **cities**, there is no
school. Now, in many places people who are not Irish also **enjoy**
this holiday.

Wind

March is a **windy** month.

The wind blows the **trees**.

The wind blows **kites**.

Children like to fly kites in the March wind.

Wind

March is known as the **windy** month. The wind blows the leaves in the **trees**. It blows our **clothes** when we walk outside. People are often chasing their **caps**. When the March winds blow, children like to **fly** kites. Kites come in all shapes and **colors**. Children run with their kites until the wind lifts them up in the **sky**. Windy days are **fun** if you have a kite to fly.

Easter

Claudia likes to **dye** eggs.

Leon's basket is filled with **candy**.

Billy has a baby **chick**.

Marcy has a **big** rabbit.

Easter

Easter is a **religious** holiday for Christians. **People** all over the world have special holidays at this time of year. Jewish people celebrate Passover. At Easter, people buy new **clothes** to wear to church and school. Stores sell Easter **baskets**. To fill the baskets, you can buy all kinds of candy and **gifts**. Eggs are made of marshmallow, chocolate, and **candy**. Many schools, churches, and the White House have Easter egg hunts. Children look for candy eggs in the **grass**.

Spring

April brings lots of **rainy** weather.

The rain helps flowers **bloom**.

Some of my favorite spring flowers are **daffodils**.

Birds build nests in **branches**.

Playing outside is **wonderful**.

Spring

Spring is the season when everything is **new**. The trees grow green leaves, and apple and **cherry** trees bloom. Flowers begin to **grow** from the ground. Animals have their **babies**. We see birds **feeding** their young. We see **new** nests being built in trees. **Gardens** are planted. The days are getting **longer**. Nights are getting **shorter**. Spring is here!

Mother's Day

I like it when my mom **reads** with me.

My mom likes to **cook**.

We play **cards** together.

We watch **television** together.

My mom looks best when she wears a **smile**.

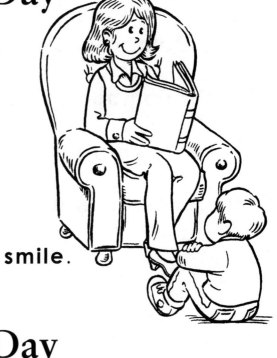

Mother's Day

Mother's Day is a **special** day in May to remember our mothers. When Mother's Day first began, people gave their mothers **cards**. Now, people also give their mothers cards and **gifts**. Many buy **flowers** for their mothers. There are special **meals** at restaurants just for mothers. We also remember our **grandmothers**. What will you do to **remember** your mother?

Memorial Day

We have a **barbecue** on Memorial Day.

We cook **hamburgers** on the grill.

We go to the **parade**.

It is a day to **remember** the veterans of wars.

Memorial Day

Memorial Day is near the end of May. It is a day when we remember all of the **people** who fought for the United States during war. Long ago, people celebrated with parades and **marching** music. Now, it is a day that many have off from **work**. Some people go to the **beach** to share time with family. Others have a **picnic**. In some **towns**, there are still parades to honor the veterans of war. In many **places** in the United States, it is the start of summer.

Father's Day

My dad can **fix** anything.

He is **proud** of me.

I like it when we **play** together.

He can **cook** better than anyone.

I like it when he cooks me **breakfast**.

Father's Day

Father's Day is a special day that **families** celebrate in June. They want to do wonderful things for their **fathers**. Some people buy **cards**. Others plan a special **dinner**. Some families have a **picnic** with hot dogs and hamburgers. Many buy their dads **presents**. My dad's present may be a new **shirt**. They want to say thank-you for all of the **wonderful** things fathers do for their families. How do you celebrate Father's Day?

Summer

Every summer we have a **break** from school.

The weather is **sunny**.

Some children go **swimming**.

Other children go on a **picnic**.

It is a time to **relax**.

Summer

There are exciting things to do in the **summer**. Some children go to **camp**. Others go on vacation to the beach. Others go to the **mountains**. Still other children find lots of things to do near **home**. They play in the **park**. They have fun at the **playground**. When they are hot, they go to the **pool**. Some children cool off in the **sprinkler**. Others like the air-conditioning at the **mall**. Many children visit the **library** or go to the movies. Many activities are planned to keep children **busy** in the summer.